PĒTERS BRŪVERIS
THE DOOR WIZARD

ARTIST
PAULIS LIEPA

TRANSLATED BY
ŽANETE VĒVERE PASQUALINI AND KATE WAKELING

A modern nursery rhyme from Latvia #004

ONE DAY A WIZARD CAST A SPELL ON A DOOR,

WHICH MEANS THIS DOOR WILL SHUT NO MORE.

CAN ENTER AND LEAVE AS THEY PLEASE, JUST SO.

THE BLANKET GOES OUT,

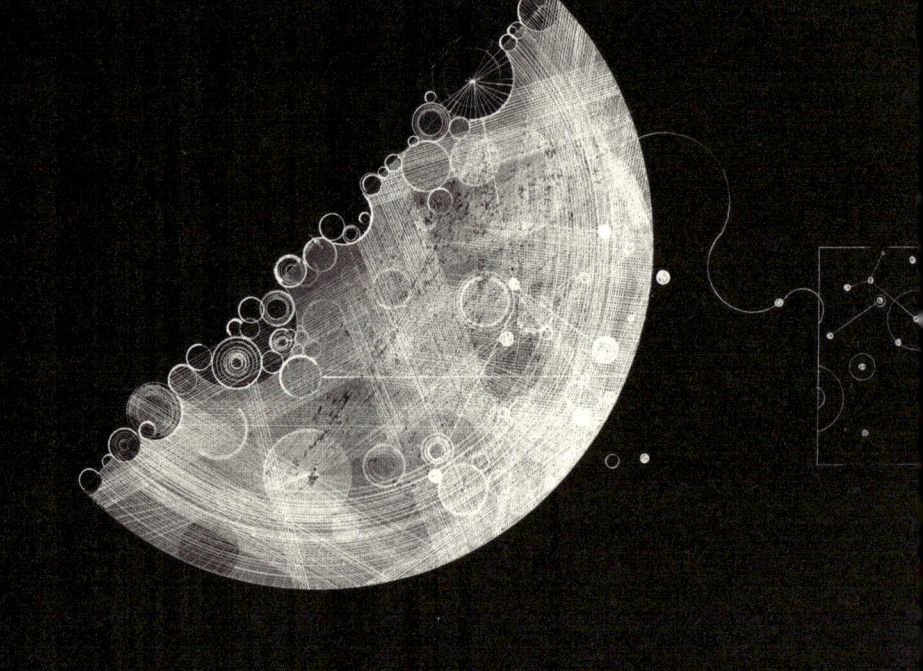

THE MOON COMES IN

WHAT SHOULD I DO?

Supported by Latvian Writers' Union (*Latvijas Rakstnieku Savienība*)
and Ministry of Culture of the Republic of Latvia

First published in the UK in 2018 by the Emma Press, Birmingham
Originally published in 2014 as "Durvju burvis" by Liels un mazs, Riga, Latvia

Text © Pēters Brūveris, 2006
English-language translation © Žanete Vēvere Pasqualini and Kate Wakeling, 2018
Illustrations © Paulis Liepa, 2014

BICKI-BOOKS
Artistic director – Rūta Briede
Design – Rūta Briede and Artis Briedis

Printed in Latvia by *Talsu tipogrāfijā*
on *Munken Print Cream* 115 gsm and *Carta Integra* 265 gsm

A CIP catalogue record of this book is available from the British Library
All rights reserved.

ISBN 978-1-910139-96-7
theemmapress.com